WRITERS AND THEIR WORK: NO 210

William Golding

by CLIVE PEMBERTON

Published for the British Council
and the National Book League
by Longmans, Green & Co

Three shillings and sixpence net

William Golding published his first and most famous novel, *The Lord of the Flies*, when he was forty-two, and since then he has published only five novels. 'Yet', writes Clive Pemberton, author of this essay, 'the importance and significance of his contribution to the modern novel is already widely recognized. He is not only one of its most distinguished practitioners; he is also one of its developers.' His formidable powers of construction and his concentrated poetic style have combined to produce work of unusual intensity.

William Golding was born in Cornwall and has lived most of his life in the south-west of England. He worked intermittently in the theatre and taught at Bishop Wordsworth's School, Salisbury, before the Second World War intervened and gave him first-hand experience of the D-Day landings in Normandy. His reactions to the war and his reflections on his pupils lie behind almost all of his subsequent writings. He has tried in his novels to trace the multitude of conflicting and dangerous passions which constitute man's nature. 'Modern man', he has written, 'is appallingly ignorant of his own nature.'

He continued to teach for several years after the publication of *Lord of the Flies* in 1954. This novel, which was later filmed by Peter Brook, struck a deeply responsive chord in the public mind and also received high praise from the critics. The second novel, *The Inheritors*, which describes the conflict between Neanderthal man and *homo sapiens*, was again highly original. His subsequent novels, *Pincher Martin*, *Free Fall*, *The Spire* and *The Pyramid*, have deepened and extended his reputation. He has also published a collection of essays, *The Hot Gates;* a stage play, *The Brass Butterfly;* and has had broadcast but not published, several plays for radio.

Clive Pemberton is a Lecturer in the English Department at Nevill's Cross College, Durham. Since graduating from Cambridge he has taught in schools in Canada and England and run an English Department for foreign students. He has an MA in Modern English and American Literature from the University of Leicester and is continuing to pursue his interests in these fields.

Acknowledgments: Our thanks are due to the publishers, Messrs Faber & Faber, for permission to quote from the works of William Golding.

WILLIAM GOLDING
by
Clive Pemberton

Edited by Ian Scott-Kilvert

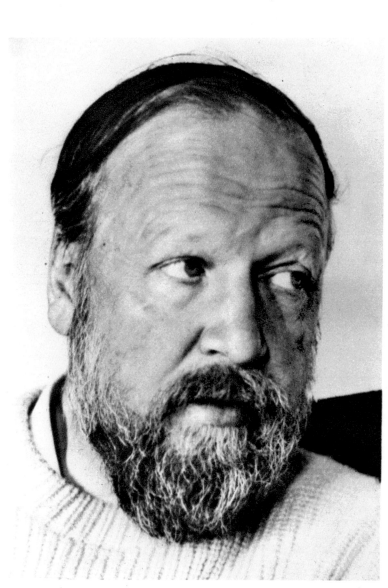

WILLIAM GOLDING

WILLIAM GOLDING

by

CLIVE PEMBERTON

PUBLISHED FOR
THE BRITISH COUNCIL
AND THE NATIONAL BOOK LEAGUE
BY LONGMANS, GREEN & CO

LONGMANS, GREEN & CO LTD
Longman House, Burnt Mill, Harlow, Essex.

*Associated companies, branches and
representatives throughout the world*

First published 1969
© Clive Pemberton, 1969

*Printed in Great Britain by
F. Mildner & Sons, London, EC1*

WILLIAM GOLDING

WILLIAM GERALD GOLDING might be described as a re-
tiring man. His public appearances have been rare
and he has tended to find his pleasures in the active
but comparatively secluded pursuits of archaeology and sail-
ing. The strong moral tone of his novels and the isolated
characters at the centre of them further suggest a grim and
uncompromising figure—an image which the warmth, wit
and humanity of some of his other writings have quite
failed to dispel from the public mind. He is not obviously a
member of any group or 'school' of writers. His short and
concentrated books demand sustained attention from the
reader and offer him writing of a kind and intensity unusual
in modern literature. He was forty-two before his first novel
was published, and he continued to teach for several years
after that before finally earning his living solely as a writer.
He has published only six novels over thirteen years, and has
consistently avoided overt comments on public issues. Yet
the importance and significance of his contribution to the
modern novel is already widely recognized. He is not only
one of its most distinguished practitioners; he is also one of
its developers.

He was born in Cornwall, on 19 September 1911, and
spent a relatively isolated childhood, during which he read
widely and developed an early interest in words. 'I had a
passion for words in themselves, and collected them like
stamps or birds' eggs . . . While, therefore, I was supposed
to be writing out my tables, or even dividing four oranges
between two poor boys, I was more likely to be scrawling a
list of words, butt (barrel), butter, butt (see goat). While I
was supposed to be learning my Collect, I was likely to be
chanting inside my head a list of delightful words which I
had picked up God knows where—deebriss and Skirmisher,
creskent and sweeside.'

He read the classics of childhood and was captured by
them—Henty, Ballantyne and Burroughs in particular. 'They
held me rapt. I dived with the Nautilus, was shot round the

moon, crossed Darkest Africa in a balloon, descended to the
centre of the earth, drifted in the South Atlantic, dying of
thirst, and tasted—oh rapture! It always sent me indoors for
a drink—the fresh waters of the Amazon.' And he read
simultaneously the classics of adulthood, developing a particular feeling for Greek literature, which he reads in the
original. 'I seem to remember that the last ten lines of book
nine (of the Odyssey) . . . came to me . . . as a sheer gift.
There were grains of sand on the page, I remember, and by
my ear the bristles of marron grass shuddered and stirred
their small funnels in the dry, white sand. With that sea
breaking on the beach, it was not difficult to lie back, repeat
the ancient words and hear the familiar surge and thunder.'

From Marlborough Grammar School, he entered Brase-
nose College, Oxford, to read science, and eventually gradu-
ated in English Literature. The switch is interesting, for it
exhibits a tension between the arts and sciences which was to
run right through Golding's life, and can be seen not only in
the shape his novels take, but in the dichotomy they often
seem to propose between rational and religious man.

There is no doubt where his major interest lay, though.
In 1934, while still an undergraduate, he published a small
volume of poems in Macmillan's Contemporary Poets
series, a series which included the work of W. H. Auden
and others whose literary reputations were to be fashioned
long before Golding's. They are clearly youthful poems,
cheerfully immature in thought and technique, and Golding
himself has wryly dismissed their claims to be taken seriously.
'I don't own a copy. But I suppose there's one somewhere.
Yes, at the British Museum. The Bodleian, too, of course.
Actually I'd rather forget it . . . You might say I write
prose because I can't write poetry.' Nevertheless, a good
number of them do, in fact, give a hint of the considerable
poetic talent evident in the later fiction, and some of them
already question the neat rationalism of the scientists and
historians he was reading at the time. There is a sprightly
'Non-Philosopher's Song'; a short, savage piece on the

death of Baudelaire which could well be an epitaph for Pincher Martin; and an excellent little poem on Pope which gives us a figure very similar to the men of Golding's fictions who are unable to tolerate the apparent chaos of Nature and human experience.

He drifted for the rest of the 'thirties, writing, acting and producing for a small, non-West End, London theatre; then in 1939 became a teacher at Bishop Wordsworth's School, Salisbury. During the war he commanded a rocket ship, saw action against the *Bismarck*, participated in the D-day landings in Normandy, and was once adrift for three days in the English channel. He did not become a war novelist, but war of some sort forms the background to at least three of his first four novels, and there can be no doubt that his war experiences were a vital part of his development. By the time the war was over he had finally rejected the confident, scientific humanism inherited from his schoolmaster father and his early environment.

He returned to Bishop Wordsworth's School and continued to write, among other things, parodies and parallels to other writer's styles, (which may partly have influenced his later development of a literary method), and four novels which were consistently rejected. In 1954, *Lord of the Flies*, having previously been turned down by twenty-one different publishers, was accepted by Faber.

The source of *Lord of the Flies* is to be found principally in *Coral Island*, the morality of which Golding found unrealistic and therefore false. The Jack, Ralph and Peterkin of Ballantyne's novel carry with them to their island the clearly delineated social and moral scale of England in the mid-nineteenth century. They lecture the natives, burn false gods, and enjoy an enviable emotional unity. 'There was indeed no note of discord whatever in the symphony we played together on that sweet Coral Island; and I am now persuaded that this was owing to our having been all tuned to the same key, namely, that of love.' A hundred years later the novelist finds that symphony more difficult to play. 'I said to myself finally, "Now you are grown up, you are adult . . . as like as not . . . the devil would arise out of the intellectual complications of the three white men on the island itself".'

On one level, *Lord of the Flies* portrays the gradual and highly plausible reversion of a group of middle-class boys into primitive and bloodthirsty savagery. To begin with, the children impose 'civilized' standards of conduct on their small community. As Jack observes, in a recognizable parody of Ballantyne: 'We've got to have rules and obey them. After all, we're not savages. We're English; and the English are best at everything. So we've got to do the right things.' They elect a leader, Ralph. They have a meeting place for discussion, and a conch shell to summon them which also becomes a symbol of rational behaviour. But the civilized standards of the twentieth century fade from the boys' minds with appalling ease. First come irrational fears: of imaginary monsters, the dark and the unknown. There is a feeling of 'something behind you all the time in the jungle'. The boys split into two groups—the hunters and those trying to retain their civilized standards—and it is not long before the hunters begin to revel in the blood-lust induced by pig-sticking. They revert to the primitive practice of painting their faces with coloured clay: Jack, their leader, feels 'safe from shame and self-consciousness behind the mask of his paint'. Finally comes the inevitable ritual chant: 'Kill the pig'! they howl, dancing round its reeking, dismembered corpse, 'Cut his throat! Kill the pig! Bash him in!' It is only a matter of time before their collective anger turns against a human victim.

Golding has said that writing *Lord of the Flies* was like tracing over the 'shape' of something which was before him as he wrote. This probably refers at least in part to the 'shape' which his thinking had taken, and particularly the 'shape' of his war experiences. But there are clearly, also, universal moral implications behind the main narrative structure, evidence of a conscious intention which existed before the

writing began and which seems to suggest an element of
'programming' in the preparation of the novel. For some it
was the modern political nightmare, a glance over the
shoulder at Nazi Germany. For others it was a conscious
dramatisation of Freudian psychology; for others an illustra-
tion of Hobbes's thesis that life without civilized restraints
becomes nasty, brutish and short; and for others still a
treatise on the consequences of Original Sin. Nor was interpretation made any easier by the highly dramatic and am-
biguous effect achieved at the end of the book when the
author, having given us Ralph's view of a God-like adult,
suddenly swings round to show us Ralph from the adult's
point of view—a snivelling little boy. For the irony takes a
further turn when the adult turns out to be like something
out of Coral Island, wearing a peaked cap and revolver, and
with the trim cruiser resting in the distance.

One of the main difficulties occasioned by *Lord of the Flies*
is that there appears to be no critical term adequate to describe its form. It operates clearly enough within the recognizable boundaries of normal fiction, yet it is also heavily laden
with allegorical significance, and achieves its most impressive
effects from what can only be described as an area of overlap,
the simultaneous operation of the factual and the fabular.
This is an unusual literary achievement, and as the problems
it poses will recur in the treatment of Golding's other
novels, and in a particularly interesting form with *The
Pyramid*, it may be useful at this point to attempt some sort
of categorization.

The most fruitful line of argument so far, initiated by John
Peter and pursued by Ian Gregor and Mark Kinkead-
Weekes[1], consists of an attempt to define the polar opposites
of 'fiction' and 'fable' and an investigation of the territory
between them. 'Fables' are those narratives that leave the
impression that their purpose was anterior, some initial
thesis or contention which they are apparently concerned to
embody and express in concrete terms. In 'fictions', on the

[1] *William Golding: A Critical Study, 1967.*

other hand, the author seeks to present a more or less faithful reflection of the complexities and irrelevancies of life as it is actually experienced. 'Fable' begins with a general idea and seeks to translate it into fictional terms. *Gulliver's Travels* and *Animal Farm* might be examples of this type of writing, and it is clear that the interest of the particular details will lie in the way they point to the generalizations behind them. *Sons and Lovers* and *Wuthering Heights* might be examples of fiction.

Obviously most novels will tend to alternate between these extreme examples. A writer such as Dickens, for instance, frequently moves between them, and a book such as *Oliver Twist* might be said to contain both elements. It is a 'fiction' in its portrayal of the criminal world; and it becomes a fable when it describes the world of the poor-house, and the people who finally rescue Oliver from that world, because Dickens is motivated in these sections primarily by abstract ideas concerning education and benevolence. Many other novels might be found similarly to move between the categories. What distinguishes *Lord of the Flies* is that it is a fiction and a fable simultaneously, and if this is so, it represents a change in the nature of the novel itself. A change of a peculiarly pure nature, moreover, as it has neither been conditioned by the ruling ideas of the age nor produced in response to the literary expectations of readers.

The question of 'form' is closely related, too, to Golding's literary style, his use of words and phrases which also operate on two levels at once. 'Flower and fruit grew together on the same tree', for instance, is a vivid statement of immediate physical reality, a factual description of part of the island. It is in the most literal sense true, and it is precisely because of this that its theological overtones are capable of being interwoven with the recurring paradisal references. Similarly, the physical descriptions of other aspects of the island, the sun and thunder, the light and shade, the water and sound, have their symbolic parts to play in the book; what strikes one most on reading them closely, however, is precisely how specific they are. The conch, perhaps the most obviously symbolic object in the book, is first presented to us with the most minute and detailed realism.

Ralph took the shell from Piggy and a little water ran down his arm. In colour the shell was deep cream, touched here and there with fading pink. Between the point, worn away into a little hole, and the pink lips of the mouth, lay eighteen inches of shell with a slight spiral twist and covered with a delicate embossed pattern. Ralph shook sand out of the deep tube.

It will shortly assume its symbolic functions, but it is first and foremost, and remains, an accurately observed and precisely described sea-shell.

It is on this sort of prose that Golding is able to erect his more ambitious effects. The echoes of hymns and psalms and the profusion of light imagery which accompany Simon to his retreat in the forest are intricately and naturally woven into the texture of the narrative. Sometimes a simple word or phrase can take on an extraordinary evocative power. 'Roger ceased to be a pig and became a hunter, so that the centre of the ring *yawned emptily*.' Coming as they do, at the sudden pause and silence just before Simon's arrival at the feast, the words 'yawned emptily' achieve a dreadful hiatus. One is suddenly aware of impending tragedy. Another type of effect is achieved, too, when the frenzied ritual is over, and the stars and the phosphorescent sea fill the scene with brightness and quiet. As the body is borne quietly out to sea, moonbeams, pearls, silver, brightness, marble, effect a kind of transfiguration, by which it is sanctified and the death becomes an elevation. This is essentially the language and the effect of poetry, but it takes off from a prose which is rooted in reality.

The prose of Golding's second novel, *The Inheritors*, which describes the extermination of Neanderthal man by *homo sapiens*, is at once more ambitious and more difficult to follow. Virtually the entire novel is related from the point of view of the Neanderthal men, and the self-imposed limitations of writing a book in which the principal characters can neither

understand nor reason about what they perceive are obvious
enough. The author has deliberately denied himself the use
of important areas of discourse traditionally open to the
novelist—introspection and abstraction, for example, are
parts of our usual mental equipment, and they cannot here
be expressed as parts of the characters' conscious activities.
As a result, the discourse of *The Inheritors* can seem strange
and obscure and occasionally even grotesque in the locutions
it contrives in order to avoid anything that might be con-
strued as reasoning. We cannot be told, for example, that Fa
cried; instead we have to perceive it with Lok, who 'watched
the water run out of her eyes'.

But the style is functional and has its expressive strengths.
It allows the author to make, without further comment, two
important and related points in his presentation of the
Neanderthalers—the limitation of their intelligence and the
quality of their innocence. We are forced to see common
actions again for the first time, and the newness becomes part
of our own awareness as we read. When one of the new men
shoots a poisoned arrow at him, and Lok 'had a confused
idea that someone was trying to give him a present', we are
involuntarily jolted out of our previous assumptions. And
because such treatment of the unfiltered sense data of these
innocents is still backed by the poetic resourcefulness of
language, such incidents as Lok's hunting for his lost mate,
or the burying by the people of their old leader, can be very
moving.

But beyond this, the point of view of the novel provides
another advantage that is perhaps even more essential, for
the limited perception of the observing characters makes
possible a mode of dramatic irony which is steadily and
cumulatively effective. In a long sequence, which takes up
nearly a quarter of the book, Lok and Fa hide in a tree and
uncomprehendingly witness an encampment of the new
people indulging in an orgy of lust, drunkenness, cruelty and
cannibalism. Here, and for most of the novel, we see the
behaviour of post-lapsarian man through the eyes of inno-

cence, and we recognize that innocence is bound to yearn towards and be destroyed by experience. It is not until the last chapter that Golding reverses the point of view and establishes a new irony as *homo sapiens*, fleeing his own inner darkness, looks back in terror at the forest of innocence, the memory of which 'may be the germ of the ogre in folk lore . . .'. The final irony is the way in which the Wellsian epigraph of the book has actually been realized.

H. G. Wells, in fact, generated *The Inheritors* in much the same way that Ballantyne suggested *Lord of the Flies*. There is his own story on the subject, *The Grisly Folk*, and more especially the eighth and ninth chapters of his *Outline of History*, where Neanderthal man is presented as an inferior creature, possibly the source of the mythological ogre of folk stories. On this, Golding has been quite specific. 'Wells's *Outline of History* played a great part in my life because my father was a rationalist, and the *Outline* . . . was something he took neat. Well now, Wells's *Outline of History* was the rationalist's gospel *in excelsis*, I should think. I got this from my father, and by and by it seemed not to be large enough. It seemed to me too neat and slick. And when I re-read it as an adult I came across his picture of Neanderthal man, our immediate predecessors, as being the gross brutal creatures who were possibly the basis of the mythological bad man, whatever he may be, the ogre. I thought to myself that this is just absurd. What we're doing is just externalizing our own insides.'

This is not, of course, strictly fair to Wells, who was aware of this kind of objection and was to emerge from the Second World War even more pessimistic than Golding. But the younger historian of the *Outline* does at times seem to suggest a philosophy in which the passage of time and the processes of education will somehow add to human refinement and accomplishment—a kind of optimism which was very common during the Victorian twilight. Golding's attack is in reality directed against the entire generation which bequeathed to him and us so many illusions. He was later to describe his father's own views as follows: 'Science was busy cleaning up the universe. There was no place in this exquisitely logical universe for the terrors of darkness. There was darkness, of course, but it was just darkness, the absence of light . . . God might have been a help but we'd thrown him out. . . .' It is this darkness from which Tuami and his tribe flee at the end of *The Inheritors* carrying it with them 'in their own insides' as they go, which is the basis of these two essentially antithetical ideas of the nature of evil—the rationalistic and the religious. It is with this darkness and the God who might have been a help that Golding is largely concerned in his third novel.

Pincher Martin does not compel a moral interpretation from the start: rather it offers a vivid survival adventure and then declares that what we have witnessed is objectively false, though it is, in fact, true in a totally different way. This is not in itself a new fictional device. *Gulliver's Travels* plays equally confusing tricks with our expectations, and the symbolical tales of Poe and Kafka work in a similar way. The difference here lies in the extraordinary care with which the author makes the apparent seem particularly real before allowing the symbolic quality of the action to appear openly. As a result not only is the reader uncertain where he stands, the ground on which he stands actually shifts within the novel, and the symbolic meaning appears in the final chapters as a completely new interpretation of something he has already accepted in a conventional, realistic way. The technical device of 'flashback', which achieves this, though normally associated with the cinema, has been employed in fiction before. Ambrose Bierce's *An Occurrence at Owl Creek* is a classic example, and Hemingway makes good use of it in *The Snows of Kilimanjaro*. The extent to which the grounds of reality change within the art form itself, however, is difficult to parallel outside Alain Robbe-Grillet's script for the film of *Last Year in Marienbad*. The following, from page two of the novel, is the moment of Martin's 'death', the desperate struggle of a dying man in the last few seconds before drowning. It is described in vivid and minute detail, seen, as it were, from inside the drowning man. Yet it contains within it, though we do not realize this at the time, the germ of most of what is to follow.

But the man lay suspended behind the whole commotion, detached from his jerking body. The luminous pictures that were shuffled before him were drenched in light but he paid no attention to them. Could he have controlled the nerves of his face, or could a face have been fashioned to fit the attitude of his consciousness where it lay suspended between life and death, that face would have worn a snarl. But the real jaw was down and distant, the mouth was slopped full. The green tracer that flew from the centre began to spin into a disc. The throat at such a distance from the snarling man vomited water and drew it in again. The hard lumps of water no longer hurt. There was a kind of truce, observation of the body. There was no face but there was a snarl.

The description of Martin's physical activity in the water has already involved the attitude of his consciousness which, if it were expressible, could be described as a snarl. In fact, his mouth is slopped full, so the snarl becomes an emblematic one, and the author is able to take up the metaphor as fact—the sailor becomes the snarling man. One aspect of the novel, at least, is a full length exploration of the difference between a 'face' and a 'snarl'. What we are offered here through the 'man against the sea' convention, just as it was offered to us in *Lord of the Flies* through the 'desert island' convention, is a system of expectations against which the author will construct a personal and different version of the 'shape' of things.

And he will construct it again largely in terms of images and image suggestions which work against the apparent structure of the book and finally undermine it. The initial courage and determination of the solitary sailor is admirable and dominates at least the first half of the book. The anti-heroic theme is eroding it all the time, but it is only towards the end that it appears openly and the adverse moral judgment is consolidated in the reader's mind. There are the Atlas and

Prometheus references and the sustained background parody of the Book of Genesis as Martin assumes command of his rock. There is the casting for the Morality play of Pincher as Greed and its subsequent linking, largely by inference and suggestion, with his meditation on the historical significance of eating and the parable story of the Chinese Box. There is the mockery of Nathaniel's patient warnings—'Take us as we are now and heaven would be sheer negation'—and the visionary interview with a mysterious figure in seaman's clothes, in whose presence the world of rock and sea stops moving and disintegrates. Finally, rock, body and mind all give way and there is left 'nothing but the centre and the claws'. Martin has asserted his own autonomy and independence; his retribution is that his premises have been accepted and realized. The final challenge to his rationalism is provided by the structure of the book itself.

But the assertive will which has throughout given Martin his heroic quality is never surrendered, and there is a sense in which the artistic impact of the book is greater than its conscious design. We are left wondering at the determination of Martin to assert himself, even in a context that makes that assertion eternal folly, almost as much as we are left meditating his damnation. What is challenged, in the last analysis, is our own inclination to admire a certain type of resolution, and our ideas of what we mean by the word 'heroism'.

The way in which Golding's books tend to transcend their author's original programme is, in fact, one of the most interesting things about them. There is an area in his novels, as there is not in the traditional construct of fable or allegory, over which the author himself has no absolute authority. This means not only that there are possible alternative readings which he cannot deny us, but that even his own views on a particular point may in a sense be inadequate.

Golding himself has said, for instance, that in his original scheme for *Lord of the Flies* the parachutist was conceived as a strictly allegorical figure; the dead man 'is' History—'All that we can give our children is this monstrous adult, who's dead but won't lie down'. In the story, however, the dead man becomes an ugly emblem of war and decay, an objective equivalent for the beast of the boys' imaginations, and many other things besides. Again, Golding's own explanation of the theological structure of *Pincher Martin* quite fails to account for the extraordinary ambiguity we are left with at the end. In both cases, and even in apparent contradiction to the author's own intention, something richer and more poetic gets into the book; something, that is to say, more various and valuable than the original scheme sets out to offer us.

Before moving on to further experiments in *Free Fall*, Golding produced a more light-hearted re-working of his seminal theme for a different medium. He dramatized his *novella*, 'Envoy Extraordinary', for radio, and later brought an expanded version, *The Brass Butterfly*, to the Strand Theatre, London, with Alistair Sim in the leading role. The spirit is lighter; the ornate dialogue of the *novella* is sharpened and re-worked for the stage; and the single-minded devotion of the Greek philosopher to Reason and Progress is intensified in the play, beyond satire, into broad caricature. The plot is probably based on Richard Garnett's short story 'The Rewards of Industry', one of the prose fables in *The Twilight of the Gods*, which mocks the confident rationalism of the late nineteenth century. Garnett, like Golding, attempts to show that the gods men worship are projections of their own desires and that the historian can measure the spiritual integrity of an age by studying the deities it invents and adores.

The philosophical essence of the play is seen when the Greek philosopher, who has prematurely discovered the secrets of twentieth century, confronts the Emperor, who has played with them like a toy and finally rejected them as too dangerous.

Phanocles: We build on the expectations of man's goodness and the foundations collapse under us . . . Caesar, I conquered the universe, and yet the ants have defeated me. What is wrong with man?

Emperor: Man. A steamship, or anything powerful, in the hands of men,
Phanocles, is like a sharp knife in the hands of a child. There is nothing
wrong with the knife. There is nothing wrong with the steamship. There
is nothing wrong with man's intelligence. The trouble is his nature!

In Phanocles we see the errors of the rational man; the
optimistic dream of a new order, in which men will behave
reasonably and in their best interests, is doomed by the
irrationality inherent in our nature. In all the other stylized
characters of the play, including the witty Caesar, we see
typical modes of rationalization which allow men to believe
that the real flux and chaos of the universe may add up to
some kind of meaningful pattern. The island, as usual, is a
microcosm, and the inane episode that occurs there reflects
the essentials of human nature and the illogicality of human
history. It does not suggest the straight line of progress the
rationalist tries to impose on human development. Nor does
it suggest any of the rewards and punishments which the
moralist or religious idealist would like to read into things.

It is these problems, the search for pattern in the universe
and the cleavage between science and religion which
dominate the next novel, *Free Fall*. The title is both a
scientific and a theological reference; it alludes to that state
of neutralized gravitational pull that is a hazard to space
travellers, and hence a part of our contemporary scientific
mythology; and it also refers to the Biblical fall from grace,
and thus implies a moral thesis. Sammy Mountjoy sees his
two 'parents not in the flesh', the science of Nick Shales and
the religion of Miss Rowena Pringle, as offering alternative
patterns of existence. Either of them could offer some sort of
solution to his problem, but both of them cannot be true.
Golding was later to write: 'Any man who claims to have
found a bridge between the world of the physical sciences
and the world of the spirit is sure of a hearing. Is this not
because most of us have an unexpressed faith that the bridge
exists, even if we have not the wit to discover it?' Shortly
before the publication of *Free Fall* he saw the basic problem

of modern man as 'learning to live fearlessly with the natural chaos of existence, without forcing artificial patterns on it', and sought to expose in the novel 'the patternlessness of life before we impose our patterns upon it'.

In some degree, therefore, the book would have to imitate the incoherence of life and, simultaneously, approach an order or design which would make it an intelligible work of art. This is certainly not the problem of the fabulist, and gives rise to an interesting structure in which events are recounted not chronologically but in order of their importance to the character who recalls them. The terrifying patternlessness which Sammy discovers finds its correlative in the form of the book, a technique which has much in common with the recent development of the 'anti-novel' in France.

One of the major exponents of the 'anti-novel' approach, Alain Robbe-Grillet, also wrote the script for *Last Year in Marienbad*, which was noted in connection with *Pincher Martin*. He, too, lays great emphasis on the extent to which humans dislike seeing their true human situation and status in the natural world, and regards the proper duty of literature today as a hygienic operation—it has to cleanse language from the 'pathetic fallacy', from projecting human emotion on to natural reality and descriptive precision. The extent to which the conventional categories of space and time can become suspect, presumably because we feel we live our space and time subjectively and not mathematically, is demonstrated very clearly by a novel such as Robbe-Grillet's *In the Labyrinth*, which carries these techniques considerably further than Golding. It is, in fact, a technical exercise in a theory of novel writing.

Free Fall, then, differs from the earlier novels in this way, and may be sharply distinguished from them, too, in the way it comes to grips with the question of environmental influence. The earlier books have been concerned to show that the perennially repeated fall of man is caused by defects in his own nature; they were thus able consciously to limit their immediate social background and in some cases practically eliminate it altogether. The everyday world of *Free Fall* is grimy, real and recognizable, and at least some of the defects in the individual are rooted in the society in which he grows up.

Sammy, too, is able to make that blind leap out of self which was denied Pincher Martin; from the solitary darkness of his prison cell he cries 'Help me! Help me!'—and 'the very act of crying out changed the thing that cried'. It does not provide him with a solution. All the hats he has tried must still remain on the wall. The two worlds of science and belief are still both separate and real, and there is no bridge between them. He remains as he began: uncertain, unsatisfied, 'a burning amateur'. His universe is still measureless and unpredictable, but at least he is more fully alive in it. In the earlier novels, we have seen typical human responses to the 'natural chaos' of existence—cardboard bulwarks erected, as it were, to shut out its terrors. However gingerly he does it, Sammy is the first to embrace the mystery.

The essays, reviews and other writings which Golding has produced, most of them between 1960 and 1962, make interesting and often entertaining reading. They are less strenuous in their demands upon the reader, and reflect the wry wit of somebody who has escaped from the teaching profession far more than they do the formidable seriousness of the novelist. One of them, however, 'On the Crest of the Wave', does deserve particular attention as something of a pointer to the Golding craft.

We are offered two 'pictures' of Education, the first a homely one from the author's family history.

I examine the History of Herodotus, specially translated for that library (The Hundred Best Books). It has slabs of small, grey print, less readable than Rawlinson, less faithful than Bohn. The liveliest, easiest, and most entertaining of histories has become a chore, a duty that only a passionate determination to be educated could stay with to the end. Yet I remember hearing of one man who read the whole library, book by book. He was a miner and a lay reader. What time he spent on the surface was devoted to the Lord's work. Yet he knew there was another sphere, apart from coal and the Lord, a sphere we might call the humanities, or culture, or education.

This is essentially expository prose and far removed from the dramatic or poetic style of the fictions. The sentences are shorter and crisper, full of monosyllables, sometimes balanced in a way that gives them a simple, and in its way, graceful precision. The lay-reader miner, too, is a simple and real enough figure; he is, in fact, an ancestor of Golding. Yet he rapidly comes to assume allegorical weight as well, working as he does at different levels and within the three separate spheres of human activity—coal, the Lord and education.

The second picture is a more formal one and is drawn from H. G. Wells again—'Education', personified as a wholesome and comely woman, kneels by two radiantly beautiful children and points to the dawn. There is no irony here; Golding willingly admits that Wells at least had some idea of what Education ought to be. It is society that has rejected the idea because 'The overtones were too vast, too remote, too useless on the national scale, too emphatically on the side of "knowing" rather than "doing".' It can be read as a contribution to the 'Two Cultures' debate, the point of correction being that we are really faced with three cultures today: the humanities, pure science and technology. And it is in the dehumanizing power of the last that Golding locates the modern evil. 'Our humanity rests in the capacity to make value judgments, unscientific assessments, the power to decide that this is right, that wrong, this ugly, that beautiful, this just, that unjust. Yet these are precisely the questions that Science is not qualified to answer with its measurement and analysis', and it is leading us 'to the world where it is better to be envied than ignored, better to be well-paid than happy, better to be successful than good, better to be vile than vile-esteemed'.

A direct result of modern priorities in education is, for Golding, a sharp decline in the ability to use and understand language. The artist who intends to maintain communication with such an audience is obliged to lower his standards, and this is precisely what has been done by a great many modern novelists. They have abandoned the richly textured language formerly expected of the literary artist, and taken up instead the bleak and limited idiom which will ensure communication with their audience. They employ the techniques of the sociologist and the psychologist, and apparently do so in the belief that these emerging disciplines are a better vehicle for accurate description and analysis of human motives and behaviour than the writer has available in literary tradition.

The 'true business' of the novelist, Golding had previously argued, is not description of behaviour or 'current affairs'. Contemporary life is only the visible expression of 'the basic human condition', which the novelist ignores at enormous cost to his art. The artist 'is committed to looking for the root of the disease instead of the symptoms', and the root of the 'disease' is not to be found in what science has taught us to call the 'objective world'; it is to be found in the observer himself, modern man, who suffers from 'an appalling ignorance of his own nature'. Thus the most vital task of the novelist today is to dramatise the life of the myth-making mind. And hence the design of Golding's own novels, so highly stylized and structured that they take on the characteristics we normally associate with poetry.

The Spire is possibly the clearest example of Golding's myth-making method. It is entirely dominated by one immense symbol, the spire itself, which is kept vividly before us and from which all the book's formal properties derive. Its construction is treated with the usual meticulous detail, while the men who build it are never clearly defined, and are developed much more through their relation to the spire than their relation to each other. There are few strong 'scenes', and those that might have been dramatically developed—the tormenting and murder of Pangall in the fourth chapter, and the death of his wife in the seventh—are drawn hazily as if seen through a mind closed by obsession. This is, of course, the mind that sees them. And the depths of man's nature are probed again through an extension of the 'cellar' metaphor, whose childhood source is recounted in 'The Ladder and the Tree', and which has also been used in *Pincher Martin* to suggest the morbidity and horror lurking beneath the conscious self. The immediate source for *The Spire* is the annals of Salisbury Cathedral, which has the highest spire of all English cathedrals. The real spire was also added, as it is in the story, a hundred years after the cathedral itself and does not appear to have been part of the original plan. Consequently the problems of construction were considerable and unusual, and the successful erection of the spire became something of an early engineering marvel, incorporating as it did many new and ingenious techniques for supporting its enormous weight. In addition, the cathedral itself was built on nothing more substantial than a spongy bog. Even the names of the two protagonists, Jocelin and Roger, are taken from two former bishops of the older foundation, Old Sarum, whose bodies lie entombed under the same arch in the present cathedral. So in more ways than may be immediately apparent the novel has its basis in reality.

The essence of the book is the conflict between Faith and Reason, but everything in it becomes increasingly double-edged. The only way to keep Roger at his task is to take advantage of his involvement with Goody Pangall. The warmth at Jocelin's back turns out to be not only an angel, but a form of spinal consumption that is slowly destroying him. Is the spire really the cold, geometric abstraction suggested by the 'diagram of prayer' formula; or might it be a phallic symbol, 'the hammer' of his sublimated lust? Might it also be born of pride? Almost everything in the book faces both ways and, although the spire stands, our only indication as to whether it stands as a monument of vision or folly, lies in the images which move throughout the novel, and particularly the images of the apple tree and the kingfisher at the end. What 'argument' there is is again conducted in essentially poetic terms, and reveals itself only through the images and symbols out of which it is constructed. 'There is no innocent work. God knows where God may be.'

In some ways, the five novels so far considered could be said to form a group. There is variety and a considerable range of technical experiment within them, but they all have behind them a firm and consistent intention—the probing of man's essential nature through the myths he invents and constructs. Myth, which reaches deep and searches for some archetypal truth, is Golding's own word in preference to fable, which he feels as something superficial, invented and on the surface. Gregor and Kinkead-Weekes, in the perceptive study previously referred to, have seen these five books as exploring 'the problem of disengaging myth from fable and giving it historical location', and suggest that with *The Spire* the tension between myth and fable is finally resolved. It is interesting, then, that Golding's only subsequent novel to date appears to set off in a different direction. It is not ostensibly a fable; it contains no evident allegory; it is not even set in a simplified or remote world. It is different; but its difference is really a difference of development rather than a departure.

The Pyramid is set in the 'thirties in a Barsetshire village, the world of Golding's childhood, and the social background is fully sketched, 'the dreadful English scheme of things at the time, a scheme which so accepted social snobbery as to elevate it to an instinct'. Within this scheme Oliver, the adolescent son of a chemist, battles with his disparate experiences: sexual violence, snobbery, artistic insight, science, (which is for him, as it was for Golding, the assigned ladder to Oxford), social advancement and a career. Within this scheme, too, the people of Stilbourne act out their thwarted impulses. They are 'all known, all food for each other, all clothed and ashamed in our clothing'. Each of the three episodes culminates in a display of post-lapsarian nakedness. Oliver mounts Evie, the local beauty, on an open ridge in full view of his father's binoculars. Evelyn de Tracy, producer of the local opera, when asked by Oliver for truth, produces a sheaf of photographs of himself dressed as a ballerina. Bounce Dawlish, the respectable ugly music teacher, walks smiling and naked into the street. And it is all written in a light, almost inconsequential style, which we have seen elsewhere in Golding, but not before in a novel.

The epigraph comes from The Instructions of Ptah-Hotep: 'If thou be among people, make for thyself love, the beginning and end of the heart.' But love, like everything else in Stilbourne society, is ambivalent; it can be torture as well as harmony, power as well as understanding. In his essay, 'Egypt from My Inside', Golding contrasts a modern pyramid of collected information, used to increase social power, with the Egyptian pyramid which 'is to be at once alive and dead, to suggest mysteries with no solution, to mix the strange, the gruesome, the beautiful'. Oliver attempts to explain to Evie the difference between information and mystery but words are not big enough. 'It's like chemistry. You can take it as a thing—or you can take it as a thing'. You see or you don't. Oliver takes Evie as a thing. He dimly perceives without actually feeling the hinted incestuous tragedy behind her promiscuity, and he understands too late: 'We might have made something, music perhaps, to take the place of the inevitable battle.'

Music is the theme of the second episode, in which the Stilbourne Operatic Society's performance of 'The King of Hearts' turns out to be a grim and very funny parody of Art. 'Art is a meeting point; but you can go too far.' It does not recognize its Dionysiac origin: 'The SOS rose from a vein which wandered through society beneath the surface. We had no ritual except mayoral processions. We had no eloquence, no display. We were our own tragedy and did not know we needed catharsis.'

In the third episode it is the stifling of sexuality for music which produces tragedy; this time in the music teacher, Bounce Dawlish, who teaches music as she inherited it, as boredom and torture: 'It is necessary to be cruel to musicians if they will not be cruel to themselves; and nothing is crueller than the position for playing the violin.' The way in which the violence of parental love can permanently influence growing lives is a major theme of all three episodes. Oliver's parents steer him relatively harmlessly from music to chemistry. But Sergeant Babbacombe beats Evie into incest; and Mr Dawlish punishes Bounce into a sterility which eventually drives her to breakdown and self-exposure. In each episode Oliver meets somebody who needs and reaches out for love, but in each case he is unable to respond. He uses Evie; he laughs at de Tracy; and he admits, over Miss Dawlish's grave, that he is glad she is dead. As he stands over her tomb at the end of the book, a 'successful' adult visiting the scenes of his youth, the image of her 'pathetic unused body' rises up before him, as a kind of 'psychic-ear-test before which nothing survived but revulsion and horror, childishness and atavism, as if unnameable things were rising round me and blackening the sun'. Yet he is unable simply to reject her as a horror and sinks into a contemplative numbness in which he does not know 'to what my feelings had reference nor even what they were'. Mystery remains the only relation between the sources of power, harmony and destruction. But Bounce's dead body, like Golding's Pharaoh's, like the Spire, is a solid object with a solid history, and we learn from contemplating it, even if we are unable to explain what we learn.

The Pyramid is not an elaborately structured book. There are certain connections of character and scene between them, but its three episodes are neither tightly linked nor obviously 'programmatic'. Reading the earlier novels and knowing something of the author's concerns may be a necessary preparation before it appears anything more than a genial, low-keyed, realistic novel of life in a small town in the 'thirties. The main Golding concerns, however, are still all there, the concluding ironies as profound and challenging as before; yet they are completely integrated into the structure, tone and setting of the book, and in no way imposed upon it arbitrarily. It is as if 'myth' has been almost entirely incorporated in 'history', and the truths of myth offered us from a basis of social realism. The 'shape' of the experience emerges at last from an ordinary social world.

This is not only a rare achievement; it is one of the ways in which the novel could develop, and one which will require all Golding's undoubted verbal and imaginative talent to demonstrate its possibilities. In due course it is possible that he may be seen to have acquired for the conceptualizing imagination a territory of operation on which its presence has always been regarded as a contradiction in terms. For the present, the work he has already produced has firmly established him as one of the most original and distinguished novelists now writing.

WILLIAM GOLDING

A Select Bibliography

(Books published in London unless stated otherwise)

Works:

POEMS (1934).
LORD OF THE FLIES (1954). *Novel*
THE INHERITORS (1955). *Novel*
PINCHER MARTIN (1956). *Novel*
SOMETIME, NEVER: THREE TALES OF IMAGINATION (1956)
—contains 'Envoy Extraordinary' by William Golding, 'Consider Her Ways' by John Wyndham and 'Boy in Darkness' by Mervyn Peake.
THE BRASS BUTTERFLY (1958). *Play*
—expanded version of 'Envoy Extraordinary'.
FREE FALL (1959). *Novel*
THE SPIRE (1964). *Novel*
THE HOT GATES (1965)
—a collection of essays and reviews.
THE PYRAMID (1967). *Novel*

Some Critical Studies:

WILLIAM GOLDING, by S. Hynes; New York and Houston (1964)
—Colombia Studies on Modern Writers. A brief but useful study of the first five novels.
WILLIAM GOLDING: A CRITICAL STUDY, by J. R. Baker; New York (1965)
—emphasizes Golding's debt to the Greeks.
THE ART OF WILLIAM GOLDING, by B. S. Oldsay and S. Weintraub; New York (1965)
—sees Golding as a 'reactive' novelist and concentrates on his 'sources'.
WILLIAM GOLDING: A CRITICAL STUDY, by I. Gregor and M. Kinkead-Weekes (1967)
—excellent and largely interpretative study of the first five novels.

Articles and Reviews

'Secret Parables', by V. S. Pritchett, *New Statesman*, 2 August, 1948.

'The Fables of William Golding', by J. Peter, *Kenyon Review* 19, 1957
—introduces distinction between 'fictions' and 'fables' in an analysis
of *Lord of the Flies*.

'The Meaning of it all', by F. Kermode, *Books and Bookmen* V,
October, 1959
—BBC radio interview.

'The World of William Golding', by P. Green, *Review of English
Literature*, I, April 1960
—particularly useful on sources of the first three novels.

'Gimmick and Metaphor in the novels of William Golding', by
J. Gindin, *Modern Fiction Studies*, VI, Summer 1960

'Distaste for the Contemporary', by M. Green, *The Nation*, 2 May
1960

Introduction to *Lord of the Flies*, by I. Gregor and M. Kinkead-
Weekes (1962)
—educational edition published by Faber and Faber. Pursues Peter's
distinction between 'fictions' and 'fables'.

PUZZLES AND EPIPHANIES, by F. Kermode (1962)
—contains good essay on novels up to *Free Fall*.

'An Unheroic Hero', by M. Quinn, *The Critical Quarterly*, IV, Autumn
1962
—useful study of *Pincher Martin*.

'William Golding', by K. Rexroth, *The Atlantic*, May 1965

'*The Spire*', by D. W. Crompton, *The Critical Quarterly*, IX, 1967.

Review of *The Pyramid*, by A. S. Byatt, *New Statesman*, 2 June 1967
—best of the book reviews.

Author's note: The format of this essay prevents me from identifying
my sources in the text as fully as I would wish. I have tried to
include them all in the bibliography.

WRITERS AND THEIR WORK

LEWIS CARROLL: Derek Hudson
CLOUGH: Isobel Armstrong
COLERIDGE: Kathleen Raine
CREEVEY & GREVILLE: J. Richardson
DE QUINCEY: Hugh Sykes Davies
DICKENS: K. J. Fielding
    EARLY NOVELS: T. Blount
    LATER NOVELS: B. Hardy
DISRAELI: Paul Bloomfield
GEORGE ELIOT: Lettice Cooper
FERRIER & GALT: W. M. Parker
FITZGERALD: Joanna Richardson
MRS GASKELL: Miriam Allott
GISSING: A. C. Ward
THOMAS HARDY: R. A. Scott-James
            and C. Day Lewis
HAZLITT: J. B. Priestley
HOOD: Laurence Brander
G. M. HOPKINS: Geoffrey Grigson
T. H. HUXLEY: William Irvine
KEATS: Edmund Blunden
LAMB: Edmund Blunden
LANDOR: G. Rostrevor Hamilton
EDWARD LEAR: Joanna Richardson
MACAULAY: G. R. Potter
MEREDITH: Phyllis Bartlett
JOHN STUART MILL: M. Cranston
WILLIAM MORRIS: P. Henderson
NEWMAN: J. M. Cameron
PATER: Iain Fletcher
PEACOCK: J. I. M. Stewart
ROSSETTI: Oswald Doughty
CHRISTINA ROSSETTI: G. Battiscombe
RUSKIN: Peter Quennell
SIR WALTER SCOTT: Ian Jack
SHELLEY: Stephen Spender
SOUTHEY: Geoffrey Carnall
R. L. STEVENSON: G. B. Stern
SWINBURNE: H. J. C. Grierson
TENNYSON: F. L. Lucas
THACKERAY: Laurence Brander
FRANCIS THOMPSON: P. Butter
TROLLOPE: Hugh Sykes Davies
OSCAR WILDE: James Laver
WORDSWORTH: Helen Darbishire

Twentieth Century:
CHINUA ACHEBE: A. Ravenscroft
W. H. AUDEN: Richard Hoggart
HILAIRE BELLOC: Renée Haynes
ARNOLD BENNETT: F. Swinnerton
EDMUND BLUNDEN: Alec M. Hardie
ELIZABETH BOWEN: Jocelyn Brooke
ROBERT BRIDGES: J. Sparrow
ROY CAMPBELL: David Wright
JOYCE CARY: Walter Allen
G. K. CHESTERTON: C. Hollis
WINSTON CHURCHILL: John Connell
R.G.COLLINGWOOD: E. W.F.Tomlin

I. COMPTON-BURNETT: P. H. Johnson
JOSEPH CONRAD: Oliver Warner
WALTER DE LA MARE: K. Hopkins
NORMAN DOUGLAS: Ian Greenlees
T. S. ELIOT: M. C. Bradbrook
FIRBANK & BETJEMAN: J. Brooke
FORD MADOX FORD: Kenneth Young
E. M. FORSTER: Rex Warner
CHRISTOPHER FRY: Derek Stanford
JOHN GALSWORTHY: R. H. Mottram
ROBERT GRAVES: M. Seymour-Smith
GRAHAM GREENE: Francis Wyndham
L. P. HARTLEY & ANTHONY POWELL:
      P. Bloomfield and B. Bergonzi
A. E. HOUSMAN: Ian Scott-Kilvert
ALDOUS HUXLEY: Jocelyn Brooke
HENRY JAMES: Michael Swan
PAMELA HANSFORD JOHNSON:
            Isabel Quigly
JAMES JOYCE: J. I. M. Stewart
RUDYARD KIPLING: Bonamy Dobrée
D. H. LAWRENCE: Kenneth Young
C. DAY LEWIS: Clifford Dyment
WYNDHAM LEWIS: E. W. F. Tomlin
COMPTON MACKENZIE: K. Young
LOUIS MACNEICE: John Press
KATHERINE MANSFIELD: Ian Gordon
JOHN MASEFIELD: L. A. G. Strong
SOMERSET MAUGHAM: J. Brophy
GEORGE MOORE: A. Norman Jeffares
EDWIN MUIR: J. C. Hall
J. MIDDLETON MURRY: Philip Mairet
SEAN O'CASEY: W. A. Armstrong
GEORGE ORWELL: Tom Hopkinson
POETS OF 1939-45 WAR: R. N. Currey
POWYS BROTHERS: R. C. Churchill
J. B. PRIESTLEY: Ivor Brown
HERBERT READ: Francis Berry
FOUR REALIST NOVELISTS: V. Brome
BERNARD SHAW: A. C. Ward
EDITH SITWELL: John Lehmann
OSBERT SITWELL: Roger Fulford
KENNETH SLESSOR: C. Semmler
C. P. SNOW: William Cooper
STRACHEY: R. A. Scott-James
SYNGE & LADY GREGORY: E. Coxhead
DYLAN THOMAS: G. S. Fraser
EDWARD THOMAS: Vernon Scannell
G. M. TREVELYAN: J. H. Plumb
WAR POETS: 1914-18: E. Blunden
EVELYN WAUGH: Christopher Hollis
H. G. WELLS: Montgomery Belgion
PATRICK WHITE: R. F. Brissenden
CHARLES WILLIAMS: J. Heath-Stubbs
ANGUS WILSON: K. W. Gransden
VIRGINIA WOOLF: B. Blackstone
W. B. YEATS: G. S. Fraser
ANDREW YOUNG & R. S. THOMAS:
      L. Clark and R. G. Thomas